Music from the Trenches

*Everything you need to know
to ensure a rich musical life
for your children*

By

Mary Jane Wilkie

ISBN: 1502336057

ISBN-13: 9781502336057

Library of Congress Control Number: 2014916495

CreateSpace Independent Publishing Platform

North Charleston, South Carolina

Dedication

I dedicate this book to the parents who go the extra mile to ensure that their children have the benefits of music.

children sing

using own voice - making music

singing reinforces our heritage, makes bonds

counters "I'm not musical"

parents who are trying to integrate the
       arts into children's lives

"mindful practice of a skill is the
       only way to develop & maintain it

(Help children decide they are capable

p. 21 intro students to operas...
   list of singable melodies

p. 28 a good songbook

Not to be overtaken by trends

exp. of parent involvement
   - help children apply themselves

present music from various musical
   traditions, explaining the best
       background & opening the mind

Use music not necessarily music
children "relate to"

Sailor off boat

offer quality - not what come then pays cullen

Acknowledgements

I am grateful to the school where I had the opportunity to know all the students mentioned in this book, and to develop my teaching and musical abilities. I thank Brooklyn College for being a wonderful place to study music. I appreciate the thoughtful comments provided by friends as I shared my experiences with them, and especially the friend whose comment suggested the title of this book.

Lai, & Jack 2

Dickson 1

Ruthie 1

Carol Amos 1

Jeanne & Don 1

Table of Contents

MUSIC FROM THE TRENCHES

Introduction

The sun shone brightly on me and my decision the day I reached the boarding school where I would spend the next six years. After twenty years in various areas of business, I was middle-aged and beginning a music-teaching career in southern California. My newly minted master's in musicology had deepened my love for music, one I would be sharing with children as young as four and as old as thirteen. Intense and constant was the thrill of having re-engineered my life in order to swim in the waters of music. I envisioned innocent faces beaming as they raised angelic voices in song. I saw young people proudly intoning the school song at graduation, parents tearful with pride and pleasure.

Unbeknownst to me, only hard work in the trenches would bring about such dream-like experiences. Several decades earlier I had taught high school, and planned to draw on that experience to teach music. The first week on the job, however, showed me how much children had changed in the intervening twenty years.

The first day I faced fifteen eighth graders who were incredulous at the expectation that they should sing with their own voices. Producing musical sounds unaided by CD or instruments was a new experience for them, one they viewed with suspicion and then dismay when they realized that I would give them a grade. And warming up voices for singing? Was I joking? They were confounded by my music choices, which were not songs they heard on TV, nor performed by groups with names like "Smashed Heads" or "Spitting Nails."

Children at the other end of the spectrum surprised me too. Eager to come to music class, these 4- and 5-year-olds didn't know how to sing, and did not know traditional children's songs. Singing games were a thing of the past, and music-making was unfamiliar to them.

How could it be so different from my childhood memories? And more importantly, what was I to do? This book describes how I figured out what to do, and what I learned in the process.

• • •

In America today, we *hear* more music around us but *make* less music ourselves, a circumstance that impacts our children in ways we do not imagine.

INTRODUCTION

There is an enormous difference between playing a sport and watching it. Those who play learn
physical skills, discipline, teamwork, and fair play.
When playing a sport, we enjoy the body's energy,
and promote its development and health. The same
is true when playing an instrument or singing. In
addition to the obvious esthetic benefits, we learn to
work with others, to be attentive, and we develop discipline. When we sing, our body enjoys the healthful
flow of air and good posture that proper breathing
promotes. We interact with the symbols embedded
in a good song text, we reinforce our heritage, and
we form bonds with others, even across generations.
When playing an instrument effectively, our every
muscle is engaged, directing the body's energy to the
production of the right sound. Many of today's children are getting none of these "whole body" benefits.

I often hear adults say, "Families used to sing. I
wonder why we don't anymore." The reason we do
not sing is that we do not sing. Making music used
to be an activity in itself. People sang at church, at
family gatherings, at camp, in pizza parlors. Siblings
learned piano duets or simple ensemble pieces. And
these were ordinary people, not families with exten-
sive music training. Music-making was a bonding,
even ritualistic, activity.

Because music-making requires *some* effort,
i.e., it is not "easy" fun, many people have ceased

developing their music potential. In addition, people hear stunning recordings by world-class artists
and cease to value their own efforts. The result is
that professionals make most recorded music, some
dedicated amateurs continue to enjoy the pleasure
of music-making, and many succumb to the notion
that "I'm not musical."

Furthermore, because many music teachers
use popular music for class activities ("music the
students relate to"), we as a society fail to develop
a common repertory of song. Many is the time I
have been in social gatherings where people had
an urge to sing, but could find no songs that everyone in the group knew. This opportunity to
bond is lost in the fragmentation of lifestyles and
musical heritage.

Should we care? Even if we do not care for ourselves, we should care for the sake of our children.
This book describes many ways to make a difference
in the musical landscape. Flooding the schools with
competent music teachers would be a good start, but
only that. Certain attitudes and habits must support
any activity society values, for the arts do not flourish merely because good teachers teach. Teachers
sow seeds. But the beds in which the seeds grow

must extend well beyond the schoolyard, to places private and public.

I once saw a sign in an art-supplies store that read "DO ART." I suspect that the creator of this sign feels about art the way I do about music. In other words, it is easy to buy images and decorations for our homes, just as it is easy to buy recordings by accomplished musicians. And while good art and music are models for quality, they are no replacement for keeping our own creative abilities alive.

Parents seem justifiably anxious today, concerned for their children's chances for success. They generously put forth efforts to prepare them for "what the economy needs." I suggest, however, that better our children be prepared for life in its richest sense. The need is not for more scientists and mathematicians, nor geniuses of any kind. Rather, we would benefit from raising children who are able to communicate, who will strive for a balanced life, and who care about one another.

To judge from issues discussed in music education journals, books, and conversations with colleagues, my experiences with children and music are not atypical. Many families genuinely want the enrichment provided by the arts. But "having the arts" in one's life comes from *doing* something rather than *buying* a product. I am writing for people who want to do something. I particularly hope my comments will serve parents who are striving to integrate the arts in their children's lives. I salute them.

CHAPTER I:

Should Children Develop Music Skills?

That we should even have to justify music is indicative of an impoverished society, but that is the subject of another book. Solid music education benefits us in many ways, from positive impact on brain development to the enrichment provided by the arts and the way they help us live. The Search Institute has identified 40 Developmental Assets, being a group of practices or circumstances that should be present in order for children to develop as happy, productive adults. I offer here some of the positive effects of music training, and suggestions for countering the obstacles to it.

Sometimes I hear parents justify less-than-diligent work in music with the comment "But Alex isn't going to be a concert pianist." A strange comment, for no one suggests that because Alex isn't headed for the major leagues he needn't give his best on the baseball field. This is so because we value sports for many reasons. One well known music director describes how he enjoys watching a baseball game, appreciating the athleticism, the technique, and discipline, and because "at ten years old I was standing at shortstop shagging grounders."[1] In other words, he appreciates the skills *he* developed by playing baseball.

Likewise, a young person who plays Beethoven sonatas, Sousa marches, or Broadway show tunes derives skills plus a lifelong source of pleasure. We develop appreciation from the execution of the activity, or as Aristotle said:

> It is impossible, or at any rate very difficult, to produce good judges of musical performance from among those who have never themselves performed.[2]

When I began writing regularly, I discovered what writers already know: I became a better reader. I noticed words, turns of phrase, and images that previously escaped me. The same thing happens with music, for creating the sounds enlivens the ears.

Esthetic appreciation is only one of the benefits derived from mastering an instrument. Others are discipline, fine-motor skills, hand-eye coordination, and some that might be classified as general wellbeing.

The brain and music
Although research had long documented the relationship between music and learning, the subject

attracted public notice in the wake of a presentation at the American Psychological Association in 1994. Researchers Frances Rauscher, Gordon Shaw, and others, demonstrated a causal relationship between music and spatial task performance. Myriad articles followed (*Newsweek*, 4/14/97, *Discover*, 10/96, the front page of *The Los Angeles Times*, 11/9/98), and continue to appear. For example, one article ends:

> With music in the brain, early humans had the neural foundation for the development of what most distinguishes us from other animals: symbolic thought and language.[3]

We should be wary, however, of misuse of data. In the transference from scientific journal to popular press, many findings become catchy phrases such as "music makes you smarter." More accurate is to say that, for example, the Rauscher study found that exposure to a specific kind of music temporarily enhances performance of certain three-dimensional spatial tasks. Another valid conclusion from such studies might well be that learners who are successful in one subject like to exercise abilities in other areas. It is clear, however, that music affects the brain, and since that time many writers have reported on the relationship between the arts and accomplishments in other areas.

The body and music

The body responds on many levels to music, in ways positive and negative, and its potential for healing has been tapped only superficially. Don Campbell's popular book *The Mozart Effect*[4] represents a small sampling of materials published on the interaction between music and the body's conscious and unconscious layers. Indeed, an entire field of study has grown up around vibration and healing. Book titles reveal the possibilities: *Healing, Imagery, and Music* (Carol Bush); *Sounds of Healing* (Mitchell L. Gaynor, M.D.); and *Vibrational Medicine* (Richard Gerber, M.D.). Their authors are conveying information about the relationship between sound and our bodies, and healing in particular.

Performance in school

Numerous studies have explored the relationship between music and performance in school (e.g., test scores, drop-out rates).[5] Whether music is the cause of these improvements is unclear. It may be that any enjoyable activity fosters growth in other areas. Regardless, it behooves us to offer children many opportunities to succeed, for strength in one area will improve a child's self-esteem overall. A successful corporate executive one told me that she attributed her success to the fact that she was a drama major. She felt that the skills, courage, and self-esteem she developed for the stage had served her throughout her life. We could say the same for music performance. Confidence and achievement in one area improves a child's frame of mind, and usually willingness to try harder in other areas.

General well being

Indeed, certain reports—usually focusing on low-income populations—state that a performing arts program can help stem violence and drug abuse. Miramax's feature film *Music of the Heart* depicted the joys and trials of a teacher who developed a strings ensemble in Spanish Harlem. I once read a report on New York City's foster-care system, which mentioned that in agencies offering performing arts, children exhibited less violent or negative behavior. This information alone seems sufficient to justify the expense of performing arts programs. Composer Marvin Hamlisch has referred to arts education as "our real 'stealth weapon' in the war against crime, illiteracy, and mediocrity."[6]

One choir director, discussing children's choirs, says:

> Singing requires stamina, both physical and emotional. Focus, sense of community, respect for others, and

> self-esteem are intrinsic in good
> quality choral performance.[7]

All parents want these qualities in their children. People who work in music and drama are acutely aware of the teamwork aspect of performance, for theatrical productions engender *esprit de corps* in cast and crew alike. Instrumental ensemble members count on one another to make the music happen. And who could fail to notice the camaraderie inherent in a good jazz ensemble? Jazz musician Wynton Marsalis made this insightful comment:

> Music is the memory of a people, their history. If you listen to the music of Beethoven or Bach, it projects much of what they thought and understood. When you're playing their music, you're interfacing with not only their great minds but with the memory of a whole group of people for whom they were the conduits.[8]

Comparing musical composition to the visual and literary arts, he says:

> Kids paint pictures and write papers, [not all] good. In fact, most of them

7

are going to be bad, but they do it anyway. By doing it, they learn how to grapple with form, how to capture their ideas in that medium, how to be expressive in that context ... and with each attempt they improve. We need to do the same with music.[9]

As in the other arts, music will benefit a child physically, intellectually, emotionally, and psychologically throughout life. Whether the child ever sets foot on the concert stage is irrelevant.

Exploration and the Imagination
I had a particularly gratifying experience with my second graders at the school one year. Several of the girls, then the boys, began to spend recess time in my classroom learning songs or playing instruments (xylophones, drums, tambourines, wood blocks, and the like). With little guidance from me, they began composing, mainly simple rhythmical pieces. There were minor altercations, some of which they handled themselves ("I think I'm better on drums than you, Chelsea"). For others they called me in ("Brad, you're not in the band any more."). For the most part, however, the children worked out their issues, performing several times for their classmates and for the entire school.

These children had captured the original sense of "playing" an instrument. That is, Mozart and company played at the harpsichord keyboard the way today's children play at the computer keyboard. They made discoveries, they enjoyed sound, they experimented, producing both good and mediocre music in the process.

In the primary and elementary grades, children should build music skills with their classmates through singing, playing instruments, and dancing. It is a time to experiment, to have fun with sound. As one writer puts it:

> Musical creativity should be encouraged in the very young, not because it is apt to produce amazing pieces, but because it gives a young student a chance to experiment with sound and begin to learn something about music's grammar.[10]

The writer means *all* young children, not just the exceptional talent (who will have ample time to grow without excessive concern in primary school). We should foster exploration, and the creativity that results from it. One writer says:

> Music is a basic part of human knowl-
> edge and experience. It should be—in
> fact it must be—a part of any comprehen-
> sive educational program for children.[11]

The "talent" question

Because I so frequently hear comments such as "she has a real gift for music," or "he is very talented artistically," I would like to address "talent." In his report "A Star is Made," Stephen Dubner posits the notion that "the trait we commonly call talent is highly overrated."[12] He confirms what all music teachers know: mindful practice of a skill is the only way to develop and maintain it.

Barring physiological barriers, all of us have *some* degree of ability in all areas of human endeavor. This is not to say that we have *equal* potential in those areas, but that each of us can develop an ability to some minimum level of proficiency. For example, even if our visual abilities are not strong, through art classes we learn basic concepts of spatial composition and use of colors. Unfortunately Americans have accepted the notion that musicality is the innate ability of some but not others. In *The Singing Neanderthals*, Stephen Mithen discusses music as a universal feature of all cultures, saying

> ... the modern-day West is quite un-
> usual in having significant numbers
> of people who do not actively partici-
> pate [in music] and may even claim to
> be unmusical.[13]

Thus, references to the talented vs. the untal-
ented are misinformed. We should encourage all
children (and adults) to develop at least a minimum
level of proficiency in all areas.

The "very talented"
Now let us consider the child who shows truly un-
usual talent, akin to Michael Jordan in basketball.
Mihaly Czikszentmihalyi says:

> Talent is best viewed as a devel-
> opmental rather than as an all-or-
> nothing phenomenon. It is a process
> that unfolds over many years rather
> than a trait that one inherits and then
> keeps unchanged for the rest of life.[14]

If a child expresses serious interest in a particular
instrument and willingness to practice, parents should
arrange for lessons. Any music teacher recognizes a
"natural." Such children learn at an astonishing rate:

SHOULD CHILDREN DEVELOP MUSIC SKILLS?

they play a figure on the violin after hearing it only a few times; they fly through the piano literature. They are a joy for the teacher, and they are very rare. Even this kind of talent should be nurtured carefully, however, for innate talent is only one of the qualities needed for success as a professional musician. Says one author:

> The extent of your child's abilities and how far his talents and energies will carry him can only be revealed with time.[15]

Support for strong interest and natural talent should be balanced with integrated development of other skills and relationships. Also, parents should take care lest the child use the ability as an escape, or avoidance of relationships. One writer says that a child may

> spend hours practicing or playing … to cope with things he cannot understand or change.[16]

Another writer warns:

> An intense musical practice schedule leads to less interpersonal practice

in negotiating, compromising and giving.[17]

History is full of stories of a prodigious talent left to develop without benefit of normal human relationships. The film *Hilary and Jackie* depicted such a story. We saw other examples of talent pushed to extremes in *The Red Violin*. These circumstances may produce a star, but I doubt it is beneficial for either the star or for society. At what price do we want to be thrilled by a prodigy?

Those of the "suffering artist" school may disagree with me, but theirs is a different viewpoint. I think the world offers suffering enough without creating circumstances where it flourishes. Helping children become more alive to the world is one of the functions of the arts. If we encourage the sensitivity to experience life in all its facets, children will have a healthier flowerbed in which to grow their talent.

CHAPTER II:

Habits Of A
Music-Rich Society

What are the elements of a good music education? Before we answer, we should consider the music-learning process and how our habits and daily activities support it.

First, assume that most children are *not* from families of musicians, so their early musical growth comes from school and any skills parents have acquired in school or church. The school's program is therefore crucial, and parental support will often mean the difference between a mediocre and an excellent program. Parents who are aware of the music-learning process, and understand that the brain and the imagination are nourished by it, can be the program's strongest supporters.

Likes and dislikes
Sometimes I hear comments such as "I don't want Zachary to hate music." If we felt this way about

math, science, or foreign language, we would elimi-
nate much of our schools' curricula. Children study
these subjects because we adults believe it to be in
their interest. Even if a child does not enjoy math,
we know that math is useful and develops the mind.
We agree that children should have some idea of the
world's history, its geography. And we know that
even if Zachary does not like P.E., he will benefit
from team sports, and from physical movement. We
can agree on the value of music if we understand
how it supports a child's growth.

Music study is two-fold: listening, and music-
making (singing or playing an instrument). Let us
consider first music-making, and some of the elements involved in the process.

MUSIC-MAKING
While music-making affects our lives in many ways,
here we will consider only the most salient compo-
nents of singing and playing instruments.

Fine-motor skills
The science teacher at the school once comment-
ed that every year his students showed increasingly *poor* fine-motor skills (he was referring to
an eighth-grade project requiring students to
manipulate toothpicks). In times past, people

developed such skills by playing instruments. In addition, children played jacks and pickup sticks, made model airplanes, women embroidered, men carved. Many of these activities have gone the way of the dinosaur. In discussing ability for the piano, one writer describes hand-eye coordination as follows:

> ...a good sense of spatial relations and a healthy capacity to acquire certain specific movements of the hands, fingers and arms. Spatial relations mean that the child can readily visualize the distance between two points in front of him. The capacity to coordinate movements means that the child can immediately sense the most efficient way to manipulate his hands and fingers so that they accomplish a series of specific moves.[18]

It goes without saying that abilities acquired through piano study improve fine-motor skills in general.

Comparing Japanese and American children, the Director of Instruction for the Yamaha Music Education Systems says:

Japanese children excel in fine motor coordination. Thus the musical materials and developmental sequences designed in Japan for the course require a fairly high degree of two-hand coordination. These materials and sequences have proven to be difficult for average learners [in the United States].[19]

Some may claim that operating a computer develops these skills, and this is probably true to a point. The reverse is definitely true: instrument players are always the fastest and most accurate typists. But computer manipulation cannot begin to approach the body coordination required to play a Bach fugue or to work with other instrumentalists in an ensemble.

But do fine-motor skills matter? Perhaps they won't in centuries to come. For now, however, it is hard to imagine a surgeon, auto mechanic, or hairdresser who could function with poor fine-motor skills. Many leisure-time activities are unfeasible without sophisticated fingers: building models, sewing, gardening, cooking, to name a few.

Discipline

Next we might look at discipline, which Wynton Marsalis equates with those of sports, along with hard work and dedication.[20] I once read that music majors in college, even if not among the *top* students, are always among the *good* students. It appears that the discipline required for learning an instrument transfers to other areas.

In today's world, unfortunately, the daily practice needed to master an instrument is not a common expectation for young people. If Zachary's friends are roller-blading while mom insists that he practice, it seems he is being punished. As a result, the only children who practice rigorously are those whose parents require it, or those whose social skills make them uncomfortable with their peers. Indeed, some children turn to music in order

> to cope with things [the child] cannot understand or change—parents who argue, siblings who tease, or a neighborhood bully.[21]

Imagine a community where *every* child knew that completion of homework (including music practice) was the prerequisite for roller-blading. The notion of punishment disappears.

Discipline has an impact on some of our more complex emotions. For example, the patience required to play the same passage repeatedly teaches one to handle frustration. The concentration involved in learning a piece for performance strengthens one's ability to focus. In fact, there are few areas of life NOT affected by discipline.

Teamwork

Every musician would agree that working with an ensemble develops a sense of teamwork and cooperation. Here is Sir David Willcocks on the subject:

> Choral singing develops a team spirit, akin to many sporting activities but without the competition. All the choir members must strive together. It has been my experience that in schools with strong music programs, the students are well-mannered and have self-discipline.[22]

Canadian Brass tuba player Charles Daellenbach, talking with a student regarding ensemble work, reported this:

> ...it was important for him [the student] to do his part right because the others were depending on him. He

would not let them down ... And there's a lot of teamwork.[23]

One need only observe a high-school marching band or youth orchestra for fine examples of teamwork.

Potential for negative experiences

A corollary in this discussion is the piano teacher who traumatizes students. More than one adult has cited this as reason for abandoning music, so it warrants comment. First, parents should be sufficiently involved to know the state of the child's emotions during the music lesson. Anyone who suspects a negative climate should attend the child's lessons. Some teachers *require* a parent to do so, a practice I wholeheartedly support. In addition to appreciating the emotional climate, the parent learns what the child is to accomplish, and can help maximize practice time.

Second, we should think about the varied ways a child might respond to a "negative" remark. Consider adult interactions. How often do we interpret a comment in a negative way, only to have a friend point out that the speaker probably meant something different? We serve children more effectively by helping them respond to comments with a positive interpretation.

My third comment pertains to character development. When a teacher expresses doubt about a student's ability, why do some children think "you're right, I can't" while others respond with "yes I can, I'll show you!"? It may be the child's makeup, state of mind at the time, or any number of factors. My own view is that one of the ways we grow stronger is by deciding that we indeed *are* capable, despite comments to the contrary.

I do *not* mean that we should subject children consistently to demeaning comments. I *do* mean that we cannot control everything that happens to them, nor can we craft their individual responses to negative experience. At best, we can help them derive positive realizations from life's curve balls.

LISTENING TO MUSIC

Now let us consider whether *listening* to certain kinds of music will cause Zachary to hate music. First it is helpful if parents' musical tastes are varied. What children hear in school also matters. In well run schools, children are exposed to thoughts, concepts, skills, and experience they would not acquire if left on their own.

Until the twentieth century, especially the advent of recording, most of the world's people heard only the music of their own village or region. Today the music of every era and culture is within our reach, insofar as it is notated or recorded. Don't we want to make these treasures available? Zachary may decide in adult life to restrict his listening to heavy metal, but we educators have a responsibility to broaden the exposure for children under our tutelage.

Love for music

Some say that a music teacher's goal is to get children to love music. While I have always hoped this would result from my teaching, I do not make it a goal. A teacher's most valuable gift is to introduce students to music that has value, i.e., has stood some test of time, or crossed some cultural line, or somehow managed to distinguish itself by speaking to many listeners. Chapter V discusses the quality issue at length, suggesting ways to foster a love for music. Suffice it to say here that good music will work its magic, even if students are not immediately aware of the effect.

For readers whose teachers presented music in less-than-interesting ways, I can only say that I am sorry the subject happened to be music. We should feel no more defensive about our field than would a Spanish, science, or English teacher. More to the point is to consider the factors that cause people to choose education as a career, and how our society can make the profession attractive to the best among us. That is the most effective way to ensure that Zachary will not hate music.

INTERPLAY BETWEEN MAKING MUSIC AND LISTENING TO IT

What about the child who, although not an emerging world-class talent, clearly enjoys music, participating eagerly in songs and dances? I hear parents say, for example, "Celeste loves music. We play CDs constantly at home and in the car." While enjoyable, this activity offers only mild support for development of music skills.

Recordings: bane and blessing

I recently observed a group of children in a music class given at a daycare center. A CD generated a song while children sang along and made hand motions. Unfortunately, none of the adults present seemed to notice that the children were, for the most part, singing random pitches, or shouting the words. That is, the adults made no attempt to help the children sing on pitch, even though the song was well within their reach. They missed the opportunity for helping children learn to generate a song with their own voices.

This scene explains the fact that many children "know" songs in the sense that they can hum a vague resemblance, but are unable to sing it on pitch, unaccompanied, accurately enough for a listener to identify.

If they constantly lean on recordings, children never develop the ability to participate fully in music-making. In discussing the difficulties of getting children to sing along in dancing games, a teacher of creative movement says:

> If you find the children balk at singing along, you are not alone. This has been an era of non-participation, and even young children seem to have lost the knack of joining in. It is immensely important, though, and needs constant encouragement from you. Stop the dance … if the children are not singing and remind them to sing. Some of them really don't know how.[24]

With the profusion of recorded music, why should one put forth effort? At the school, when teaching a song to my youngest students, I often found that children were familiar with the song because "my mommy plays a CD." Rarely did they answer "my mommy and I sing it."

Urging parents to sing with their own voices, one mother says:

> Today, young mothers are routinely presented with lullaby tapes at the baby shower. When baby cries, the idea goes, they will be able to switch on the high-tech audio system and the little one will drift off—the voices of strangers in his ears, perfectly on pitch.[25]

Infants and toddlers love to hear mom or dad singing to them. It is a way of bonding, and will set the stage for development of music skills. I even read of one mother who quieted her son's tantrums by singing to him!

From personal experience, I can attest to the power of music to soothe an unhappy child. I was visiting my niece, whose 3-month-old often cried, even though she was well fed and changed. Sitting with other family members, the child began to cry, and I started to sing "This Little Light of Mine." My brother and sister-in-law joined in with harmony, as did my sister, and we watched in amazement as the child ceased her weeping and listened for the entire thirty minutes or so that we sang.

The joy of rituals

When I was young, part of the in-car activity on long trips was singing. We learned songs, recalled songs, created songs, and enjoyed the singing of them. Mom and Dad knew the songs too, and the general family sharing remains with me today. Music played a vital role in our family traditions.

We humans are more ritualistic than we realize, and children value family ritual. If we want to be intentional about music and rituals, we must unplug the playback device and start singing. Others may not join in immediately, and in the absence of a common repertoire, it will take time to establish singing as a valid and valued activity. It is well worth the trouble, however, and the next section offers some suggestions.

CHOOSING GOOD, SINGABLE MUSIC

Good song material abounds, although much of the material marketed as children's music is not singable. Reference to an earlier time will help explain this comment.

When music was transmitted orally, melodies had to be easy to remember, which means interesting, and pleasing to the ear without benefit of accompaniment. The best examples of good singable melodies are folksongs, i.e., melodies not attributable to any composer, and persisting over centuries.

I refer here to *true* folksong, as opposed to songs written by a known composer in the style of a folksong (e.g., Woody Guthrie, Joan Baez).

Strong, lasting melodies

In the 1960s, much popular music ceased being singable. Or even if easy to sing, was not interesting. Two Beatles songs will serve as example. Stripped of its instrumentation, "Lucy in the Sky with Diamonds" is not an interesting melody. By contrast, "Hey, Jude" is a pretty melody, singable with only minimal or no accompaniment. This is not to say that "Lucy in the Sky with Diamonds" is bad music, only that the melody does not stand alone, but rather requires harmonies and instrumentation to be pleasing.

Singable melodies are attractive without benefit of instruments. They hold up when you add instruments, or sing them in different styles. Exemplary is centuries-old Gregorian chant, where each naked note enhances the preceding note and prepares the ear for the note that follows.

If our children are to sing enthusiastically, they must have singable melodies. In my classes, I have always relied on folk tunes, and songs that have longevity. Here are a few examples from the abundance of folk material:

HABITS OF A MUSIC-RICH SOCIETY

Skye Boat Song

Li'l Liza Jane

Frère Jacques

Dona Nobis Pacem

Kum-bah-yah

The Ash Grove

Make New Friends

Hush, Little Baby

Johnny Has Gone for a Soldier

Arirang

Nobody knows the trouble I've seen

Loch Lomond

Arroz con leche

Oats, Peas, Beans and Barley Grow

Here are examples of good melodies by known composers:

Bicycle Built for Two

Grandfather's Clock

Oh! Susanna

K-K-K-Katy

You are my sunshine

Take me out to the Ballgame

Meet me in St. Louis

When Johnny comes marching home

Supercalifragilistic-expialidocious

Introducing children to these songs yields rich rewards, for they will sing them spontaneously, never tiring of them. If we did no more than reacquaint ourselves with the existing body of good music, we

would have material for a lifetime. I suggest therefore buying a good songbook with traditional tunes,
which has the added benefit of connecting us across
generations. Imagine the delight a child feels learning a song that grandma knows. And isn't the song
dad used to sing dear to our hearts?

Giving our children good songs nourishes them
for life, for a good song is rich: instructive like a book,
warm like sunshine, cool like a stream, as appealing
as laughter, a light in the dark, relief from anguish.
Songs are, after all, poetry set to music, and we all
know the potential of good poetry to move us.

The act of singing feels good, because we are
breathing. Note that when anxious or startled, we
hold our breath. When we sing, we breathe, we
feel safe. I think that adults are often moved by the
sound of children singing because at that moment
we feel that nothing bad can happen. Why not have
many of such moments?

FROM SONG TO INSTRUMENTS

If children learn to use the first instrument (the body,
the voice), they will be better prepared for those that
evolved later. The earliest instruments were adjuncts
to body sounds made as part of ritual, e.g., rattlers or
shakers to augment the sound of slapped thighs or
feet stamping the earth. Drums are almost as old, the

first being hollow tree trunks struck by hands (sticks evolved later). Instruments that sound because the player blows through them (aerophones) also belong to these early levels of human evolution.[26] Reeds and bones, after all, can easily become flutes.

Young children and instruments
Children's early experience should be with non-pitched percussion instruments (drums, rattles, shakers, scrapers). They should enjoy a "bang-bang" stage while still toddlers. Blowing on horns, kazoos, and then recorder, provides an easy segue into more complex instruments. Children love to play with instruments, will pick up any that look interesting and experiment with its sounds. The parent or teacher should give direction to this creative play, so that as young ears and imagination become more sophisticated, skills will develop in parallel. Specialists in early childhood education mention these stages:

1. Sensorimotor Music Behaviors
2. Exploration Music Behaviors
3. Construction Music Behaviors
4. Games with Rules.[27]

Indeed, a child will exercise muscles with instruments, then consciously explore, then construct patterns, then evolve to games with parameters. Playing with simple instruments lays a valuable foundation for learning, and it is useful to be aware of how these stages support one another. As proficiency increases, the growing child will need structured support, so that physical skills keep pace with the child's increasingly sophisticated ears.

Private lessons

When the child expresses interest in individual lessons, parental commitment is being summoned to a new level. How should parents respond? Here are some thoughts to guide the move to private lessons.

I often hear parents say "Albert begs for piano lessons, but we'll get an electric keyboard and see how motivated he is." Although an electric keyboard is a useful tool, it is *not* a piano, no matter what the salesperson says about weighted keys and settings of "grand piano" or "honky tonk." Parents owe it to Albert to give him the real sound. But the "real sound" varies. No one would expect a ten-year-old Volkswagen to feel, handle, or perform like a brand-new Mercedes. Pianos are no different, and the $200 spinet the neighbor is selling or giving away will not sound the same as a Kawai studio upright, or a Steinway concert grand.

Parents might consider this comment:

> If your child's first instrument is near-
> ly a toy, or in poor condition, it will be
> difficult for her to sound good. That
> is not only demoralizing, but actually
> hinders progress. On the other hand,
> being able to play an instrument that
> sounds pleasing, even if not first-rate,
> contributes to self-esteem and is a
> great incentive to continue.[28]

The goal is to get the best available for one's bud-
get, consulting one of the various books available
on piano purchase.[29] If tying up funds is an issue,
rental is an option, and most stores will apply rental
towards cost of purchase. It is not unwise to pay
the additional sum required to rent a brand-new instrument. Speaking of new band instruments, one
writer says:

> You will also eliminate the pos-
> sibility of hidden dents or cracks
> or leaks which make playing the
> instrument dramatically more dif-
> ficult and frustrating. A major
> cause of first-year dropouts ... is

the discouragement and inconvenience of an instrument that needs
frequent repair.[30]

The practice dragon
Instrument acquired, we face the motivation issue.
All learning begins with the novelty phase, when
the learner is sufficiently intrigued to devote a lot
or even excessive time to the new pursuit. At first
Albert will relish time at the piano, be excited about
his lesson, and even begin to show creativity by
composing melodious fragments. As his involvement deepens, however, he will discover (not consciously) that unstructured application, inconstant
and non-sequential, will generate only sounds that
he has heard before. It will be difficult for him to
produce more interesting sounds without a higher
level of skill, and of course, the discipline required
to develop to that level.

The "fun" of practicing
Former Juilliard faculty member Herbert Stessin
makes this point:

> As with anything else, students will
> not learn enough to *enjoy* playing
> without a certain amount of work

and discipline. If teachers let a child
coast, little progress will be made
[emphasis mine] [31]

Parents can help children apply themselves in a
way that is not unequivocally "fun," but rather satisfying. Sinichi Suzuki, creator of the enormously
successful Suzuki method, in referring to the prow-
ess of a young violinist, said:

It was a result of circumstances that
he played the violin. Whether he
liked it or disliked it is not the ques-
tion. Precisely as all Japanese children learn the Japanese language,
and learn it by heart, to like or dislike
it had no bearing at all.[32]

Notice how children struggle with reading until
they can read for enjoyment. It is the responsibility of parents and teachers to support children (even
prodigies) to the threshold where their skills enable
them to enjoy music-making.

Parental involvement is so important
that we could speak not just of the
child prodigy, but of the child-parent

unit. And the teachers … form a part
of the unit.[33]

Compare the adult learning experience. How
often do people take up a pursuit (sailing, winemak-
ing, language study, or painting) only to abandon it
when they realize what is required to reach a higher
level of skill? This behavior supports a consumer
economy, but sets a poor example for our children.
By contrast, learners who persevere cross the threshold where the activity becomes satisfying and not
merely instant fun.

Family support for young musicians
The "difficult stage" preceding the threshold need
not be arduous. If the activity is valued by family
and friends, the confirming of each step will give
the child a sense of accomplishment, and the process
itself will be valued over the result. This means that
family members should notice and applaud when
the young pianist has achieved something, e.g., can
play an entire piece.

Activities that *prepare* a child for music learning are useful as well. At recess at our school,
children would regularly play "four-square," a
game that causes them to develop skills useful in
soccer. When old enough to try out for the soccer

HABITS OF A MUSIC-RICH SOCIETY

team, they had a foundation. Music offers the same potential, i.e., there are games and activities that support the development of music skills, even if children are not ostensibly making music. Some of these (such as language play) are described in Chapter IV.

Another form of family support is not allowing children to abandon a pursuit. A six-year-old joined our "small strings" class at school one year. After the first lesson she complained to her mother about holding the tiny violin in playing position. What is a parent to do? If supportive, the parent will encourage her to try for x minutes, then 2x minutes, and so on, secure in the knowledge that the teacher's demand is not excessive.

On another occasion, a five-year-old wanted to discontinue violin lessons after three classes. A wise parent will realize that the child does not understand the implications of quitting, and will insist that the child continue to at least the first recital. Parents can help the child by starting and ending commitments in an intentional way, making it clear that a newly purchased violin represents a commitment for an agreed-upon amount of time.

Children need constant encouragement in the music endeavor. Regarding practicing, Roberta Markel says:

> It is an error to consider a child's abil-
> ity to practice by himself as a test of
> his interest in music. Many children
> are dependent for a long time on the
> active cooperation and approval of
> the older members of the household.[34]

And here's what one middle-school student said about learning:

> One thing I have learned [from
> studying music] is that you have to
> stick with something once you start.
> … It takes a lot of work to play well,
> but the work always pays off.[35]

Fortunately, we have enough adults willing to support children through this phase. This is why today we have orchestras, chamber ensembles, and bands.

If Albert begins to consistently resist practicing or going to lessons, parents should probe for reasons. If the parent confirms that the teacher is doing a good job, other factors might need adjustment, for example, an older sibling who teases the child about a "sissy" activity. If that troublesome issue is addressed, rather than quit, the solution might be to continue until reaching a certain level of proficiency. My mother's method was to insist that we complete the program year. That is, when at summer's end we were pressing her for piano lessons, she would agree, on the condition that we continue until the following June. We were under no obligation to start piano lessons in the fall, but once we did, we knew it was a commitment until summer. This arrangement seems to work for many families.

Choice of instruments

Albert may want to change instruments mid-stream, and parents may be tempted to say "perhaps the flute is really his instrument." My own view is that the child should stick with first choice until reaching the threshold mentioned above. Otherwise, Albert will complete the novelty phase on various instruments without really learning to play any of them. Mastery of one instrument easily transfers to another, but learning only the rudiments of various instruments does not develop solid skills.

Worthy of trust is the primal attraction to one sound versus another, and the instrument should be the *child's* choice, rather than what a parent played when young, or always wanted to play. It is crucial to develop a foundation in *some* instrument, for proficiency in the first will support learning the next.

It is also important to develop a sense of musicality, and a good teacher exploits every activity to that end. For example, playing scales in a mechanical way is boring to listener and player alike, but making scales sound varied and interesting is a valid music task. *Making sounds musical* is the activity, regardless of instrument.

Family interaction

The task for adults is to help children apply themselves. Many adults did not get such support, to judge from comments such as "I started piano as a child but didn't want to practice and my mother let me quit. I wish she hadn't, because I'd be able to play today" (Dad is never to blame, by the way).

I once read an interview with soprano Dawn Upshaw, who referred to singing corny tunes with the family. Indeed, family music-making is in the life of many professional musicians. My fervent hope is that parents participate formally and informally in their child's musical development. Many avenues are available. The parent may learn along with the child, attending lessons and practicing the various exercises. The child will be thrilled to reach a level surpassing the parent. Another way is to play duets with the child, either on the same instrument, or on the flute the parent played in high school years ago. Another way is for the family to sing to the child's piano or guitar accompaniment, which is especially pleasurable at holidays. Parents will find their own ways, for there are many, limited only by imagination. Families that play together stay together.

Technology And Musical Computers

What about the newest player on the music field: the sound-producing computer? It can imitate the sound of instruments, which pipe organs have always done. It can keep a beat, thus replacing the metronome. In other words, technology is not new. Promotional literature and advertising would have us believe that because students are excited about technology, learning is improved. But is this so?

Music in the body

Consider the situation in which the student uses a digital tuner to tune the guitar. Tuning may be finer than that achieved with the student's ears, but developing the ear to hear intervals is crucial to good playing. Just as we want a child to understand addition and subtraction before using a calculator, we should insist that the child understand basic notions of how music is put together before logging on at the terminal. This means how to use rhythmic, melodic, and harmonic patterns in meaningful ways. It also means feeling music in the body.

It is not uncommon to see a "music classroom" where children program the computer to provide a rhythmic backdrop, or specific harmonic progression, and then play a melody. Are they "making music"? Am I climbing a mountain if a crane is at the summit, hoisting me up the slope as I run my hands over protruding rocks? I reach the summit, but how much have I done myself?

The founder of Patagonia, Inc., discusses this issue in connection with the equipment they manufacture for climbing. In *Climbing Ice*, Yvon Chouinard describes how, at a particular stage in the evolution of the sport, new tools made it possible to climb almost any slope in the world. His feeling was that the sport would benefit from replacing these tools with greater skill and courage:

> I felt that the whole idea of climbing should move away from goal-oriented technology to a place in which personal qualities like creativity, boldness, and technique were supported rather than suppressed by the tools of the trade.[36]

The comment applies to music learning, for unless the entire body is engaged in meaningful, stimulating, creative ways, children think they have "made music" when in reality they have acted only as ornaments on the computer's performance.

Music is a full-body activity

In the nineteenth century, when the metronome was new, Brahms wrote in a letter: "The metronome has no value ... for I myself have never believed that my blood and a mechanical instrument go well together."[37] While it is clear that the metronome can be useful in music learning, Brahms's observation reminds us of the importance of feeling the beat in the body, the physicality of music-making. As with the digital tuner, it is not a substitute for development of the body's internal ability.

I once performed a Scott Joplin rag on an electric keyboard. Although the sound was set for "grand piano" and the audience applauded, I sorely missed the physical act of engaging with the acoustic instrument, feeling its vibrations. Playing an electric bass with a pick does not produce the same sensation as hugging a bass fiddle while plucking the strings. Setting an electric keyboard to play a melody with a clarinet sound is quite different from playing a clarinet.

One educator suggests using phenomenological analysis to know what is gained or lost in the acoustic vs. electric experience. Musicians my age have experience with the physical sensations of acoustic instruments. Our children often do not, and will not experience music-making as a whole-body activity unless we decide to make it so.[38]

Technology: crutch or tool?
How can we use technology as tool rather than crutch? Some ways are easy and obvious. As with language labs, a computer can handle mechanical work, to reinforce classroom learning. For example, ear-training programs spare the teacher one of the tedious tasks, leaving more time for other activities during class.

Any technological advance results in a gain and a loss. Notation is efficiently and cleanly done with software these days. Lost is the music-learning derived from notating or copying by hand. Such software enables students to compose using instruments they are not able to play. This is a gain when compared with the pre-computer age, when orchestral composers would imagine the mesh of instruments, with no opportunity to confirm until a live orchestra played their score. The loss is in development of auditory acuity.

Computer programs allow working at one's own pace, repeating drills as often as needed, using tutorial programs that are well-sequenced, as well as the possibility of interacting individually, in groups, or as a full class.[39] Schools should keep *musical* objectives in the forefront, however, and refrain from applying technology until the gain is clear and present.

The goal: musicality
We should remember that the computer teaches nothing about musicality. The challenge is to know which technology supports learning, and when to apply it. Ear training routines to supplement class work are very valuable, as are programs that provide historical background on a particular piece of music. Resources abound, but teachers should opt for those that do not create the illusion that a student is making music when this is not the case.

The lure of technology
It may be helpful to place computer-assisted learning in the framework of technology in general. We seem eager to let technology handle everything these days, looking only at the labor saved, while ignoring the benefit lost. One obvious example is the automobile. We gained enormous mobility but

lost the benefit of physical activity, paying for it with pounds of flesh, literally.

Browsing once in a bookstore of a national chain, I was distracted by a voice talking about the great outdoors. Treading my way through the aisles to the source, I found a forest ranger addressing six people seated no farther than fifteen feet from the lectern. In that circumstance, an amplified voice was unnecessary, and a distraction for us browsers. The alternative would have been for the speaker to project her voice, generating energy to engage the audience. In my view, this would have been preferable, for an energized voice is attractive (and the skill can be learned).

During my ears at the school, I had an ongoing debate with colleagues about the use of microphones at student assemblies. Students were in the habit of speaking into a mike held beneath lowered chins while reading from a card to an audience located no more than twenty feet away. As a result, potentially interesting presentations were rendered ineffectual, because students never looked at the audience as they mumbled into the haven of the microphone. Teachers would justify the technology, saying, "children can't talk that loud," forgetting the volumes reached when children *want* to be heard.

I had the opportunity to demonstrate otherwise, when my seventh-graders once gave a presentation on drums. To introduce our improvised percussion piece, four of the boys were to describe the uses of drums in various cultures. As they stood up to speak, a teacher extended a handheld microphone. The first boy refused, saying "Nah, I don't need it," as if to say "real men don't use mikes." The others followed suit, projecting and enunciating beautifully (I could have kissed them). Children flock to technology because adults do.

Rather than create a dependence on technology, the better plan is to help children energize their voices, to work with them on enunciation and elocution, much the way teachers did when declamation was usual in schools. Children who grow up speaking before their peers and elders will necessarily develop a strong public presence and the self-confidence that comes with it.

The value of the human presence
Another issue is the use of recorded music as background for singing, which is common today at school performances. This often happens because no pianist is available to play (or no funds are available to pay a pianist). The practice is detrimental to music learning because the performers become more attentive to the mechanical source rather than benefiting from the human interaction that is part

of the fun of music-making. One music educator says:

> Some choral directors have found tapes useful in the learning process and even use them to teach parts. But as a substitute for a live accompanist in performance—thumbs down![40]

An unintended but negative result of recorded music is that student musicians learn to de-value what they themselves produce, comparing their own output with that of a professional studio. My students often harbored this notion, and thought that recordings would enhance their singing. It took no small amount of time to convince them of the value of their own lovely voices raised in song.

Performances in a school setting exist to serve the learning process, not to entertain the audience, although the latter is often a result. Children should present what they are capable of presenting with their own resources. A well known director of children's choirs makes this comment:

> ...the psychological benefits of music performance: as a way children have of confirming their existence, as

> a means of developing self-esteem, as
> a tool for adapting to life in modern
> times, and as a means of developing
> sensitivity to inner feelings.[41]

If we have more music around us today, but make less music ourselves, technology is not to blame. Why let technology supplant our own efforts when much of the joy of music-making is in the group interaction? If we continue to detach ourselves from our bodies, one day we may not need the latter.

Sometimes, when seated at the computer, mouse under palm, I have a nightmarish vision: human beings with huge heads and withered limbs, doing their work with only slight hand and eye movements. Perhaps the future of music lies in this direction: pushing buttons to synthesize the sound of an instrument. But then why would we need instruments? Just as "upper-case letters" are so called because capital letters resided in the typesetter's upper case, we would have a "clarinet sound" and only those interested in the history of music would trouble to learn the origin of the sound.

Is this cause for worry? No more than is genetic engineering or space flight. It is our responsibility to use technology in beneficial rather than detrimental ways.

CHAPTER IV:

Adults: Recapture The Joy And Support Your Children

Adults often deny themselves the joy of music-making, for many reasons. First is lack of confidence in one's own ability. A single negative or sarcastic comment has discouraged many an amateur singer.

Second is the notion that music is for the professionals. This idea manifests itself in areas besides music: "If I'm not a poet [that is, I do not publish my poems], I have no business attempting to capture my feelings in poetic form." Fortunate are those who value the process of wrestling with feelings through an art form.

The blessing and curse of recordings

Reinforcing these circumstances is the wealth of top-quality recordings, performed by musicians who spend their lives polishing technique and learning repertory. Our own "production" can seem unworthy by comparison. It might surprise readers to know the degree to which recording studios edit music, in effect making a "perfect" rendition appear to be the norm.

There is the joke about two well known musicians sharing a cab to Carnegie Hall. Emanating from the radio was music that caused one to say to the other, "Hey! That's you playing! Boy, I wish I could play that well." The other responded, "So do I."

Tone deafness: fact or fiction?
Attitudes and practices conspire to convince ordinary mortals that they have no business lifting their voices in song. The adult who says, "I can't carry a tune in a bucket" misunderstands, for (with minor exceptions) anyone can sing. One noted researcher and educator says:

> There is a common belief that a person is born either a singer or not a singer. That is not true. Barring physical disability, every child can speak and every child can sing. The ability to use the singing voice has no more to do with music aptitude than the ability to speak has to do with intelligence. [42]

Commenting on the same phenomenon, another educator says:

> Almost every adult who considers himself a listener [only] has been talked into that state early in life by an inconsiderate and ill-informed parent or teacher.[43]

Such adults tend to treat their children's ability as though singing were an inherited trait, thus inalterable. I have worked with many "tone-deaf" adults and children to help them hear a pitch, then sing it. They then begin to sing intervals, and from there, simple melodies. Suddenly, they are singing!

As with any skill, some are born with better ability to distinguish differences in sound. *Everyone*, however, can develop the ability to distinguish one sound from another. Here are comments from those who have researched the matter:

> Just as there is no person without some intelligence, so there is no person without music aptitude.[44]

> All children possess musical abilities that can be nurtured through instruction.[45]

Physical production of sound

Sound is vibrations, and a given pitch is sung by passing air through the vocal cords at a specific frequency. What the ear hears, the voice can imitate. The act of singing uses muscles to engage the vocal apparatus in specific ways. Correct pitch, dynamics, and pleasing quality are then achievable through practice.

A softball metaphor helped my students understand that singing is learned. If on one's first throw the ball does not reach the plate, no one says "I can't pitch." One tries again. If it is difficult to place the ball in the imaginary rectangle between the batter's shoulders and knees, one keeps trying, training arm muscles to respond to what the eye perceives. In singing, we cause vocal cords and diaphragm muscles to respond to what the ear hears. In softball, the body responds to a visual target; in singing, the target is aural.

The magic word: practice

So how do we help ourselves and our children learn to sing? The more we hear singing, and the more we sing, the better singers we will be:

> Good singers develop through frequent listening and then by replicating the sound of the singing model.

> Even the more powerful and reso-
> nant young singers are likely to have
> developed their abilities through
> practice, singing regularly because
> they enjoy it.[46]

With the knowledge that most people's ears function quite well, one writer describes learning notes this way:

> The sound must be *attended to*;
> The listener must have a method of
> *coding* the sounds;
> The listener must hold the various
> sounds in a *structure* or *pattern*; and
> finally, The listener must translate
> received information into a *response*.[47]

Children or adults labeled "tone deaf" have not completed the process, but music pedagogy offers ample suggestions. They may be as simple as closing the eyes, listening to a pitch played repeatedly while consciously hearing it, then singing the pitch. With one pitch sung accurately, the next one is possible.

The singer can then work on intervals (the distance from one pitch to the next). A good music teacher helps students with the more difficult intervals until they become easy. Thereafter, it's just practice, practice, practice. This doesn't mean that everyone will have a gorgeous voice, but *every*one can match pitch and keep the beat.

When I was young, we had lots of practice, singing at church, at camp, at home. Readers may remember the "bouncing ball" at the local movie house. While awaiting the feature film, we would see song lyrics projected on the screen. A white ball would bounce over the words in the appropriate rhythm, and the audience would sing along. We sang at other public places (Shakey's Pizza, if memory serves). In such circumstances, no one was dissuaded from singing, and we sang with gusto.

Today, however, I hear comments such as "whenever I would sing, my husband would turn up the radio. So I stopped singing." Unfortunately, discouraging words come from music teachers as well. Many adults recall with resentment a teacher who told them to mouth the words. While I sympathize with the teacher's desire for good sound, we teachers should not opt for the easy solution. Rather, we should work with students who have trouble. It is well worth the extra effort, and is, in my view, not optional.

Time was when people sang merely because they felt good. In my family, we knew all was well when my father was singing around the house, for whistling and singing were little expressions of satisfaction. When not overridden by recorded music, small children sing spontaneously, making up songs as they play. If we are to re-learn singing, we must be children, unembarrassed when our happiness shows.

MAKING THE HOME SOUND

A music-rich home life is supported by priorities, attitudes, and habits that create a situation where the arts flourish. The habits of a bygone age served music well. Rhymes that family members would say and sing to infants prepared them for music learning, for word play, for literature and drama. I remember a rhyme my mother used with babies. With a child seated on her lap facing her, she would raise and lower her knees alternately, saying:

> Old mule goes walk, walk, walk, walk, walk;
> Little pony goes trot, trot, trot, trot, trot;

Big horse goes gallopty, gallopty, gallopty, gallopty, gallopty.

With each line her speed increased, and by the
time she approached the "big horse" part, her knees
would move together to support a child bouncing
and giggling with delight. We loved this game, and
did not know that it was a lesson in rhythm, beat,
and tempo. My mother had no special music training; she was just doing what *her* mother did. In a few
years, we had graduated to Mother Goose rhymes,
chanted, sung, danced, and acted.

The rhythms of language

Language has rhythms; its rhythms are energizing
and rich in learning opportunities. Listening carefully, we can detect rhythms in everyday life. The dance
company Stomp! has developed stunning rhythmic
performances from ordinary sounds. Children who
develop curiosity about, and love for, sounds of the
universe more readily respond to music.

Here is what a neuropsychologist has said about
the importance of nursery rhymes:

Why are nursery rhymes so important? Not only do they get children
"hooked" on listening to language,

but they also teach valuable skills. It's the patterns, the rhythms," [the librarian] explains, "the way language is put together so pleasantly. Patterns are the most important for early reading—and even for math. Putting letters together in patterns, learning that everything in the world goes together in patterns—that's so important for the little ones."

Reading specialists tell us children's ability to discriminate and create rhyming words, as well as their sense of rhythm, are closely related to early reading ability. A child who has absorbed over and over—through the *ears*, not the eyes—such common word parts as "fun, sun, run" or "fiddle, diddle, middle" as well as the melody of their language is statistically destined to have an easier time learning to read. [48]

My father enjoyed playing with everyday sounds. I remember watching him use a handsaw to cut a board in half. He would say to us, "Listen, it says 'Wilkie, Wilkie'." We listened, and indeed, as he pushed the blade back and forth, the sound resembled "Wilkie." We were thrilled by this observation. It was just one of my Dad's ways of amusing us. There are no bounds on what we can do to make our lives musical, so I offer the following suggestions merely to illustrate.

Most important is to sing with our children, in the car, at home, at picnics, at the beach. Play an instrument, join a choir. *Sing* Christmas carols instead of listening to them. If there is no pianist or guitar player in the family, find someone in the community, and invite them to join the gathering. Memorize a favorite poem and say it slowly and often. Pronounce the consonants cleanly to get the maximum benefit. Enjoy its images while saying the words. Good poetry makes effective use of the natural sounds of a language: its cadences, its inflections, its mix of vowels and consonants. Every child should hear good poetry, for songs are, after all, poems set to music.

A people's music is closely allied with the sounds of its language. Here is a comment from an ethnomusicologist:

> [use of] speech and contour pattern
> in spoken language communication
> plays an important role in defining

> the underlying accent and contour
> pattern in the music of [that] culture.[49]

Chants that children recite and dance to will help them develop a sense of music. The world's people have always had singing games, have always accompanied chants with rhythmic clapping, stamping, finger-snapping, and other body percussion.

Take any Mother Goose rhyme, Shel Silverstein poem, or Kipling's poems from *The Jungle Book* and chant them, then set these imminently singable poems to music. Do not be ambitious about creating a melody. Try working with only a few notes, ones children can sing. "Hot Cross Buns" uses only three notes. "Amazing Grace" is a pentatonic tune, that is, it uses only five pitches.

Everything in life is a song cue, and songs have been written about everything. Learn songs about things that matter, about what is important. Make sounds for the sheer pleasure of feeling them in the mouth, hearing them in the ears. We should not deprive our children or ourselves of these experiences.

And let us celebrate the music-makers: take the children to concerts of classical music, jazz, Renaissance madrigals, Japanese taiko drumming, Indian ragas. Take them to hear grand opera, reading the stories before attending. Learn about bluegrass music before hearing a performance. Let children tour an old movie palace to hear its theatre organ. Ask a church organist to show the children pipes of the organ. Visit a bell tower and feel the vibrations as the bells ring (read Dorothy Sayers *The Nine Tailors* to know their deadly strength).

Set priorities that support these activities. Decide that money spent on pianos and music lessons is a wiser choice than other options, and that practicing is a valuable activity. Decide that the rehearsal time with a community chorus has more value than other options. Make your values known at school to parents, teachers, and administrators. Insist that the school's music program ensure a good music education for our children.

MUSIC AT SCHOOL

Spurred by reports that "music makes you smarter," schools today are revisiting the notion that the performing arts offer developmental opportunities. While this is a positive trend, it forces parents and administrators to grapple with the daunting task of evaluating school music programs that are irregular at best and poorly staffed or non-existent at worst.

Misunderstanding prevails about what "good music education" means, and the music-learning process is not self-evident. Adding to the confusion is the abundance of methods for educating a child musically.

Before one can evaluate, however, a program has to exist, i.e., music classes and performances must occur regularly and frequently at school. Occasional entertainment by performing arts groups does not constitute a program, nor does an occasional field trip to the symphony. Some schools hire artists-in-residence to give a block of music classes over several months. Even this cannot begin to build the skills required for solid music learning. Surveying the state of music programs nationwide, one commentator said:

> It remains doubtful how many school pupils are receiving the kind of *consistent, sequential* exposure to music that can produce real results.[50]

If, however, music is offered year round, here are criteria for assessing the program.

"Raw materials"

First, consider the "raw materials": teacher, time, and equipment. Is the music teacher first and foremost a performer, or does he or she have training in music education, and if so, what kind? Schools often hire performers to teach music, which does not in itself ensure quality instruction. A performer will be a good educator only if he or she has (or acquires) the skills to *teach* music, *and* has a sense of commitment about helping children learn.

Beyond university music-education degrees, music pedagogy has benefited from methods referred to as Orff, Dalcroze, and Kódaly. Developed by three different European musicians/educators in response to specific conditions, these methods have proven invaluable to music educators who strive for excellence. Most good teachers have training in one or more of these methods.[51]

Next, look at the time devoted to music each week. Although the effective educator will get valuable mileage from any time available, a thirty- or forty-minute weekly class is hardly sufficient for building solid skills.

Consider also the music materials used in class and for performance. As is the case with all the arts, junk abounds. In music, "junk" means materials that are not challenging or nourishing, music that no one will remember in a year or so. For quality, look first to folk melodies, and music that has stood the test of time. As one educator has stated:

> Our grandparents' songs and rhymes
> have continuing value: they are filled
> with wonder, they blend words and
> music expressively, and they are still
> delicious after many singings.[52]

The text must be good poetry, so as to enrich the language experience. One music specialist says:

> Good lyrics have poetic value. They
> say something worthwhile and say it
> well. As a general rule ... "If it's not
> worth saying it's not worth singing."[53]

Quality is of course present in all cultures, and materials should include music from many lands, thus exposing children to variety in musical characteristics as well as viewpoint.

The last raw material is equipment, or instruments and space. Is there a separate music classroom at the school, and if so, is it adequate for the task? What instruments are available to children? Since the dawn of time, people have made music using everyday objects, particularly the human body, and no one was ever prevented from making music by lack of manufactured instruments. But any school promising even a minimal introduction to music should have simple percussion instruments. In fact, some methods were developed using specific instruments (e.g., Orff). Although an effective educator will function well without those instruments, the class is better served if the school has them.

The school may use computers to assist in music teaching, although this in itself does not ensure effective learning. As mentioned in Chapter III, the issue is whether the technology supports the objectives of the program, especially *musical* objectives.

Classroom activities

Of course the educator must use raw materials effectively and with ease. Parents should observe the teacher's work, to see whether the music classroom is a joyful place where true learning occurs.

Next to consider are the music program objectives. If children are to reap the many benefits of music, the emphasis must be on music-*making*. That is, children should sing, play instruments, and move or dance, rather than engage in quasi-music activities. One music specialist says:

> ...lessons should be built around
> actual musical experience, not just

drills, musical crossword puzzles, or
teacher-talk *about* music.[54]

Do not consider a school's program inferior if it
does not include sight-reading from notated music.
It may be that, with limited time, the teacher has set
priorities that exclude reading. One music educator
comments as follows:

> Music literacy [i.e., reading notated
> music] can and should be developed
> ... but we need to achieve a realistic
> balance in our curricula. When lit-
> eracy becomes the primary objec-
> tive, much of the time may be spent
> drilling simple songs with simple
> rhythms and tone sets. There may
> not be adequate time left for students
> to discover great literature that is
> notationally too complex for literacy
> study.[55]

Reading notated music is valuable, but should
not have the highest priority. As with foreign language learning, the student who generates musical sounds will have little trouble transferring such
knowledge to notated music, but the reverse is not

true. Also, some methods (e.g., Kódaly) make use of rhythmic notation and hand signs. While less complex than full notation, these practices allow children to respond to symbols with music sounds, and offer a base for later music reading.

Listening to music is valuable if structured and based on good music (see Chapter V on quality). Listening time, however, should be balanced with music-making. Singing is essential in a good music program. An effective teacher takes time with those who need help matching pitch and learning to hear themselves. A good teacher will also ensure that students sing with their best voices, as opposed to the "shout" singing prevalent at so many school performances.

In the classroom, the teacher's voice should not be a crutch as children learn a song, nor should the piano. One music teacher suggests a sometime rehearsal with no accompaniment, finding that this is often the only way for students to learn their parts well.[56] Good music educators withdraw the support of their own voices at the appropriate time, and they have students sing a melody without piano support (even when piano accompaniment is planned for the performance).

The teacher should believe that music-making is for everyone, not just the "talented." Any child can achieve a minimum level of proficiency, and the teacher should strive to bring everyone along the path of joyful music-making. Children with good tonal memory, an innate sense of rhythm, or excellent ears, will progress on their own and need not be the focus of the class. June Hinckley, former President of the Music Educators National Conference, says:

> The challenge is to engender a significant level of engagement in all participants, not just the talented or those who have rich musical backgrounds.[57]

Performances

Most children love to perform, and self-confidence and composure are obvious benefits of performing. Not all music class time, however, should be a rehearsal for the next event. First, our children are better served if they develop enjoyment for the *process*: a love for sounds, for musical qualities inherent in good poetry, for the pleasure of working with their classmates. Second, the better their music skills, the less rehearsal time will be required in the long run.

I read with amazement the story of a teacher who replaced a longtime teacher whose bands had won many awards. The replacement teacher was stunned to discover that band students essentially played the same half-dozen tunes year after year. The former teacher had taught them by rote and drilled them day after day. Most of the students had no ability to sight-read even the simplest music. These students were not learning music skills; they were simply rehearsing 100 percent of the time for the next performance.[58]

The resulting mix of raw materials and worthy objectives becomes apparent at performance time. In addition to improved singing, children will demonstrate good performance habits: stand erect, focus on the conductor, keep hands out of pockets, take a good singing stance. They look and feel proud when doing so.

"Cute" children

One notion about small children is so prevalent as to deserve comment. Adults often say, "Children look so cute on stage." Children look cute doing almost anything. I once saw a performance of "The Twelve Days of Christmas" where children in costume did nothing more than wiggle their bodies whenever their "character" was mentioned in the song. They were very cute, but capable of much more.

In a performance worthy of the name, a student will demonstrate an *acquired* skill. The chief value of a school performance is that is promotes development of the *performer*, rather than entertaining the audience (although the latter is the result of a good performance). One highly respected children's choral director stresses the importance of:

> [Replacing] the concept of "performance" as a public concert, or a public relations vehicle, or school entertainment with a *new* concept of "performance" as a *way of educating children musically through active participation in the production of music.*[59]

When "cute" is the goal of performing, we do our children a disservice, for it takes neither skill nor practice to be cute. Better we should realize that even very young children can learn simple motions, songs with easy intervals and narrow ranges. By working with age-appropriate yet challenging materials, they build a foundation for more advanced music and dance later on.

Suzuki-method students constantly demonstrate what is possible with a small child. Any reader who has attended a performance prepared by a music educator with solid training in Orff, Kódaly, Dalcroze, or any of the other serious music pedagogies has witnessed a performance based on solid acquisition of skills.

Elements of a good performance

What constitutes a performance that is true music-making and satisfying to children and audience alike? Most important is that materials be age appropriate and right for the skill level. For example, although young children are often able to sing *along* with many songs beyond their age level, their performances should feature songs they "self-generate." This means songs a child can sing on pitch, in rhythm, with no accompaniment or recording (even if accompaniment is used during the performance). For dance and movement, simple motions performed on cue or accurately within an ensemble are more indicative of skill than is random shuffling by children attired in glittery costumes.

The program should avoid recorded music if at all possible. With the short supply of good general pianists, this may be difficult, but is well worth the trouble. An older student or an adult playing simple accompaniment on piano, guitar, or autoharp is preferable to studio-produced elaborate background music. One music educator says this about the use of canned music for performances:

> I do not think it is good music edu-
> cation to use accompaniment tapes
> in performance. It not only deprives
> the conductor of any sense of musi-
> cal artistry, it also deprives student
> accompanists of the opportunity to
> develop their skills. I have also no-
> ticed that when choirs use taped ac-
> companiments, the students tend not
> to follow the conductor—they follow
> the tape. As conductors, we want our
> students to become more responsive
> to conducting gestures, and tapes do
> not aid in this objective.[60]

I am puzzled by the extent to which lip-syn-
ching is accepted in school performances. Parents
would recoil at the notion of a calculator-solved
math problem presented as their child's work. And
they would not accept a photograph in which a computer overlays an image of their teenager on a rock
the child did *not* climb. Why endorse such falsifica-
tion in music?

Let the children present what they are able to
perform comfortably and the performance will be
awe-inspiring. The experience will also be satisfying for the children, for they know the difference

between manipulation of adult sentiment and an honest demonstration of their own skills.

In schools today, students' music ability is hardly ever developed to its fullest, because of time. An effective educator will, however, set attainable goals, all the while striving for a balance among the various elements of music (melody, harmony, rhythm). My minimum goals for all students at the school were: keep the beat, sing on pitch, and cooperate with their classmates in music-making. These modest goals are attainable in almost any circumstance, and produce true music-making.

Action to support the program

What should parents do if the school's music program falls short? First is to locate like-minded parents, then make the collective thinking known to the administration. The school's director may share the parents' views and need support. Make parental wishes known to other school administrators and to public officials. Become aware of legislative initiatives affecting the arts.

While waiting for the school's program to grow, parents might consider private lessons.[61] Group music-making tends to be more joyful, however, so another possibility is to locate a studio that offers basic music skills for children:

> Many good music schools and pri-
> vate teachers offer appropriate
> group lessons for very young chil-
> dren. These classes ... usually meet
> once or twice a week, for about a half
> hour ... They are very informal and
> allow each child to take what he or
> she can from the experience. These
> classes give the young child an op-
> portunity to explore and experience
> the various elements of music ex-
> pression: rhythm, melody, harmony,
> dynamics, and form.[62]

Some of the more well known programs are Kindermusik and Musikgarten. These programs are cropping up everywhere and are easy to find on the internet.

In all cases, parents themselves should make music: sing with the children (*sans* cassette or CD player), join a chorus or choir, dust off the trumpet from high school band and resume practice or les-sons. Children value grownup activities and will develop a positive view of concerts if parents attend regularly. Children should join parents at concerts, and not only classical music. Hear performances of Celtic music, barbershop quartets, operettas, Indian

MUSIC FROM THE TRENCHES

ragas. These are only a few of the myriad traditions that delight and nourish us, and we owe it to our children to offer them these sounds.

CHAPTER V:

The Case For Quality

How do we assess quality? As with literature and the visual arts, good music engages us throughout our lives and across generations. Some songs disappear after one season, yet others persist over centuries. Quality music stands the test of time, and speaks to many listeners, even across cultures. Today's hip music is usually tomorrow's castoff.

I faced the quality decision early in my tenure at the school. I had been away from schools for some twenty years, and children and young people were not the picture I retained from earlier times. Exposure to myriad activities, the relative ease of travel, the availability of information, all worked to give them an aura of sophistication. They were not "childlike." Also permeating the school culture was the notion that teachers did not automatically command respect.

MUSIC FROM THE TRENCHES

Should adults be hip?

My first year at the school brought me in contact mostly with seventh and eighth graders, energetic adolescents flexing adult muscles by using phrases whose intent or context they are only beginning to grasp. I had to decide whether to strive for coolness in my school persona and in the music I chose.

I saw that what I planned was quite different from my students' usual fare. In fact, the music in my lesson plans could not hold a candle to the music of groups with names like "Lead Freaks" or "Destroyer Five." I considered investing in a black leather outfit. I toyed with the idea of full-body tattoos and piercing each ear five more times. After visiting and revisiting notions of value, I decided not to be hip, and have never regretted it.

As I have described in other chapters, America was a singing nation when I was young. At school and in church, we sang songs from our history, much of it folk, the rest lyrical pieces that because of their singability and interest had withstood the test of time. It was music sung by past generations and it served in many ways as ritual and connectors to other times.

In the home we kids had our own space, with the then-new 45-rpm record player. We sang with gusto about the "one-eyed, one-horned flyin' purple people eater," and the "big panama with a purple hat band." We were passionate in our devotion to the Everly Brothers and Buddy Holly, but it never occurred to us to perform our music at school, church, camp, or with parents. I remember those songs fondly, but would never turn to them for nourishment.

Spiritual nourishment
When in life we struggle, confront, challenge, resolve, persevere, and feel, we seek help from various sources. Quality music, art, and literature given to us at any stage of life contain nuggets of wisdom whose potential to transform, to enrich the spirit, is realized only as we mature. Not producing fruit immediately, these nuggets are seeds waiting to germinate. They will make their presence felt at the appropriate time, when a life circumstance does not yield to easy, pragmatic solutions. It is not that popular music is bad, but that its effectiveness lies in its ability to amuse and entertain rather than nourish us in difficult times.

In referring to his youth, Boston Pops Conductor Keith Lockhart said:

> I used to go home from my piano lesson and turn on the Stones and the Who. I still enjoy the stuff I grew up

> with and I still listen to it, but I don't
> think I ever confused what I played
> on the piano and what I listened to on
> the radio in terms of lasting value.[63]

I once saw a mother refrain from sharing her church's wonderful old hymns with her teenager because "even though they are so meaningful to me, he just doesn't relate to them." Forgotten was that when *she* learned them, she did not "relate to" them either. Only after she had experienced struggles in life did their value become apparent. If we know the worth of a song, a hymn, or a poem, we should give them to our offspring, even if they don't initially see their value. Would we refrain from giving them Shakespeare because they "don't relate to it"?

Good music, art, and literature will serve them in life, even though the value is not apparent until a life circumstance evokes its message. One prominent music educator offers this comment:

chewing gum for the eyes

> Commercially imposed "ear candy"
> gives a temporary rush but lacks the
> lasting nutritional value of the litera-
> ture whose place it usurps. If chil-
> dren are to develop healthy bodies,
> they must be nurtured with healthy

food and exercise. Similarly, quality language usage and literature affects children's speech, vocabulary, reading habits, and musical growth.[64]

In the visual realm, C.S. Lewis comments on the effect on the soul of a well-designed visual object:

> The visual concentration [on a symbol] symbolizes, and promotes, the mental. That's one of the ways the body teaches the soul. The lines of a well-designed church, free from stunts, drawing one's eyes to the altar, have something of the same effect.[65]

"Nourishing" art teaches the soul, and this is related to the "God" issue. All good art is religious, in the sense that its symbolism is powerful enough to join us (re-ligare) to something greater than ourselves. As the mention of God provokes anxiety in education today, let us consider the arts and religion.

The God question
Artists depict what they believe and perceive, producing their art out of love either for the things of earth or

the things of heaven. Like religion and advertising, art uses symbols to bring about an effect. If the symbols are meaningful and skillfully presented, the viewer or listener will be transformed. We all need symbols to help us live, to guide our understanding of life's perplexing events. Rituals based on timeless symbols transform us in ways that verbal expression cannot.

Consciously or unconsciously, we daily absorb messages portrayed in symbol. Those not from quality art usually come to us from popular culture. We should consider whether we want the media to determine our children's entry into the symbolic world, and how intentional we want to be in our use of ritual and symbol. Our actions in this realm will have lifelong effects on our children.

My second year at the school, a teacher requested help preparing an assembly program on Thanksgiving. She was uncertain how to acknowledge the holiday in song without mentioning God. I perused songbooks for Thanksgiving music devoid of religious reference. The only piece I found included the lyrics: "Take out your musket, take out your gun; gonna' have a turkey shoot, gonna' have fun." In other words, guns, yes, God, no.

That incident helped me decide *not* to choose music based on the absence or presence of God. I reasoned that the pilgrims were in search of religious freedom, and they regularly gave thanks to God. Since God was so much a part of their lives, one should either acknowledge the deity or not celebrate Thanksgiving. I chose "Now Thank We All Our God," a hymn dating to the time of the pilgrims, and the children sang beautifully. No one was thereby converted to Christianity.

The presence of God in song looms large in the minds of many, and adults often censor themselves rather than risk a comment tainted with belief in a deity. When their only response to the issue is to banish materials that might possibly be construed as religious, children are rightly confused.

In its position paper on religion, the Music Educators National Conference has stressed the importance of including music of all styles, forms, periods, and cultures.

> Since music with a sacred text or of a religious origin (particularly choral music) comprises such an important place in the history of music, it should and does have an important place in music education.[66]

To what extent do we become what we sing? If my students sing a Native American prayer to the

Morning Star, does this make them believers in the
divinity of that celestial body? If a chorus sings
"Nobody knows the trouble I've seen ... but Jesus,"
have the singers accepted Jesus as Lord and Savior?
Does singing the Hallelujah chorus foster belief in
the sovereignty of God? I am sure the entire clergy
wishes it were that easy.

A noted music scholar and educator has pointed
out:

> Just as it is possible to study Com-
> munism without indoctrination or
> to examine the ills of contemporary
> society without promoting the seeds
> of revolution, then it must also be
> possible to study sacred music (with
> performance-related activities) with-
> out parochialistic attitudes and sec-
> tarian points of view.[67]

We would never deprive our children of the opportunity to view Michelangelo's *David* or the *Pietà*.
Nor would we remove reference to Christ in hell from
Dante's *Inferno*. Could we read Faulkner's *Absalom,
Absalom* or T.S. Eliot's "Journey of the Magi" without
reference to their Biblical sources? The MENC paper
includes the statement:

> [S]tudying painting without those
> with scriptural themes, architecture
> without cathedrals, literature with-
> out mention of the Bible, or music
> without sacred music would be in-
> complete from any point of view.[68]

Traditions

Parents often complain that children's only interest in Christmas is the presents. I suggest that we're not giving them any other message. By the second winter at my school, I was impatient with student questions such as "Why should we sing Hannukah music since we're not Jewish?" I was weary of comments about singing Christmas songs. I decided to cover both traditions in preparation for the school's annual campus-lighting ceremony.

I discovered that (with some exceptions) students identifying themselves as Jews were rarely informed about the history of Hannukah (who Judas Maccabeus was, for example). Nominal Christians did not know why we celebrate Christmas. While learning "O Come, All Ye Faithful," a student asked why we couldn't learn something tradition-al. What did he mean, I wanted to know. "Oh, perhaps 'Rudolph,' or 'Grandma Got Run Over by a Reindeer'." The more I sifted materials for songs and stories familiar to my students, the more I realized that their "traditions" consisted mostly of whatever was featured on TV that year.

With the conviction that singers should understand the subject of their songs, I read to my students about the Maccabees, and about the Nativity. For older students I prepared a worksheet giving the historical background of Hannukah and of Jesus, and quizzed them. Many did not know that Jesus was Jewish.

We discussed belief in terms such as "those who tell the story say the lamp burned for eight days," and "Christians believe that Christ was the son of God." Everyone learned songs about dreidls, menorahs, Christmas trees, Bethlehem, wassail. I taught them about the imagery surrounding the winter solstice, source of many Christmas traditions. A few complained that they believed nothing, so did not wish to learn any of the material. I suggested that they should act with integrity and not take a Christmas vacation (an idea not well received).

Frustrating is the hypocrisy surrounding Hannukah celebrations in schools. Lavishing attention on what is a minor (and non-religious) holiday in the Jewish faith, we ignore the high holidays of Rosh Hoshanah and Yom Kippur. I suggest that we do so because Hannukah falls near Christmas, and we can be multicultural without too much inconvenience.

The value of symbols

The symbols of Christmas and Hannukah are very old, offering light in a time of darkness. The use of evergreen boughs, holly, ivy, and mistletoe to ward off evil dates back many centuries. People have long lit candles to restore the dying sun of the winter solstice.

Belief in God aside, these are powerful symbols. Our children long for ways to understand the world, as do we adults. A good song offers some combination of history, language enrichment, and life lesson. We need the spiritual comfort provided by good music and well wrought poems and stories, whose images engender a new perception, and foster hope. Artists are in search of beauty, which is one way of looking at God. Quality art, effectively used, has the potential to cultivate a desire for goodness and beauty in our children. I suggest that children's lives are thereby improved, as are ours.

Students and choice

Unfortunately, rather than mine the rich lode of good music, many teachers today let students choose the performance pieces, fearing that "they won't like my choices." In the guise of giving them a choice, we in effect restrict them, for what they "relate to" is but a miniscule representation of the world's music.

MUSIC FROM THE TRENCHES

Unless students are aware of the full array, they perforce choose from what they know (thus no real choice). In addition, what teens reject at first they often begin to enjoy in the learning process.

With these convictions I began developing the music program at my school, with materials intended to convey concepts, to develop listening skills, and to enrich lives through study and performance. What kind? Rather than categorize music as classical, jazz, or popular, I found it useful to choose from a rich cornucopia of music "traditions." My ever-growing list appears below. We can derive pleasure and nourishment from all these musics, and need not restrict ourselves to only one or two. Young people, even more so children, know nothing of categories, and for the most part simply respond to music.

bluegrass, gospel, Renaissance dance music, Dixieland, big band, bebop and jazz of various types, Indonesian gamelan, African talking drums, rock and roll, barbershop quartet, Indian ragas, Middle Eastern belly dancing, madrigals, mariachi, Andean, blues, various Caribbean traditions (reggae, calypso), marimba band, Brazilian samba and batucada, Welsh choral music, rags, Sephardic, Scottish bagpipes, Irish tenors, Broadway show tunes, theatre-organ music, Renaissance lute pieces, Russian choral music, Judeo-baroque, early American tunesmiths, hymns of the Protestant church, Celtic, Gregorian chant,

THE CASE FOR QUALITY

Jewish liturgical music, songs from the Auvergne, English boy-choir music, Korean drums, tango and other Rio de la Plata genres, flamenco, Portuguese fados, klezmer, Gilbert & Sullivan, brass bands of America and England, piano music from the romantic era, concerti grossi and other baroque genres, oratorio, grand opera, symphonies and string quartets, songs and chants from geographic regions spread throughout the earth, and (true) folk tunes from everywhere

My decision to use music materials other than what students "relate to" produced gratifying results. For a listening assignment, I read the story of Orpheus and Eurydice to a seventh-grade class. We discussed the underworld and I showed them images by artists such as Gustav Doré. I played selections from Gluck's classical opera of 1762, *Orfeo ed Euridice*. We heard the music for the Furies and for the Land of the Blessed Spirits, then the heartbreaking "Che farò senza Euridece!" We discussed how the musical characteristics of each supported the story, which story fascinated them. They debated whether they would have looked back, causing Eurydice to die. One boy brought in a picture of Rodin's *Orpheus and the Furies*. In short, they loved both the music and the story, for teenagers are nothing if not romantic.

Another year I taught the eighth grade to sing Bach's "Bist du bei mir." Although initially they resisted singing in German, they surprised themselves by their own ability. This peaceful song with its beautiful melody expresses the singer's desire to have a loved one near at the moment of death. One boy asked how one could be peaceful when dying. This led to a discussion of the way various cultures view death, and what might have been the experience of dying in the days before hospitals.

To a seventh-grade class I told the story of Gilbert & Sullivan's *H.M.S. Pinafore*, interspersed with musical selections from the operetta. Although not immediately attracted to the images of Victorian England ("they look so weird"), these brassy teens were soon caught in the spell of the music. One morning recess the entire class barged into my room to sing "When I Was a Lad." They then gleefully raced off, certain that they had altered my day (they had). Whenever I would pass members of that class on line for lunch, inevitably the boys would intone "I am the Monarch of the Sea." They loved the goofiness of the *Pirates of Penzance* plot, and sang along with "I am the very Model of a Modern Major-General."

One year I taught my eighth graders to sing "The Water is Wide" (Waley, Waley). Although they were initially scornful of its sentiment, the song quickly won them over. I know because a teacher told me she heard some of the girls singing the song on a hiking trip. These smart-mouthed adolescents were always left in thrall by the love duet from *Porgy and Bess* ("Bess, you is my Woman now"), so affected were they by the song's lush sounds and sincere emotion.

I could give additional examples, but those cited confirmed my conviction that if we choose quality music, trusting it to do its work, it will not fail us.

One additional comment: I learned to stop treating teens as a monolithic body. It is usually the most outspoken who make disparaging remarks about music that is not "theirs." Their peers may or may not agree, but since no one wants to be different, they *appear* to be of one mind. Most teens and preteens absorb indiscriminately whatever material is presented, regardless of quality. This holds true for food and television as well as music. We should give them quality, that which will not come their way through the popular culture that is their main source of art.

It is ironic that for the first time in history, all the world's music is available on recordings, yet many continue to hear only a small selection from only one culture. If we sow only one kind of seeds, and they are ordinary ones, we will grow only one kind of flowers, and ordinary ones at best. We owe our children more.

Epilogue

Since I left California, I have worked sporadically in music education: music director for high-school musicals, private piano lessons, children's theatre. I have realized that it might not be possible for me to teach in many of today's schools, for a variety of reasons.

Articles abound on "teacher burn-out," and readers may attribute it to class size, poor pay, or excessive administrative work. These factors matter, but the *real* reason I'm not teaching is that parents (and often school administrators) expect me to accept behavior *they* tolerate at home and in public places. Sometime in recent history, many parents became incapable of disciplining their brood, or setting boundaries for behavior in the home and in public.

You know these situations:

- A child careers around in supermarket aisles, with no admonition from the parent to settle down.
- While mom chats with another adult in a restaurant, her child bangs his fork on the table,

the clanging relieved only when the waitress takes his fork away.

- Parents storm the principal's office to protest a D on the report card (the student has failed to do the simplest homework, despite many opportunities).
- The principal dismisses children from a school assembly, and bedlam ensues as they charge off to homeroom.
- A 12-year-old engages with an electronic device while an adult is speaking to her, or she walks away mid-conversation.
- A young piano student decides mid-year that he doesn't feel like it any more, and parents allow him to stop lessons.
- A mother complains: "I told her ten times to clean up her room." Once should be enough.

Why the unwillingness to enforce the desired behavior? Concerned that their direction will be perceived as harsh, parents (and many teachers) fail to convey expectations and fail to apply consequences for non-compliance. I am not the only one to observe that many children are disrespectful to adults, loud in public places, and lacking in self-control. It should come as no surprise that some restaurants do not allow children as guests, and parents seem powerless to control their offspring in those settings.

EPILOGUE

Some adults say, "they're just kids, what can you expect?" Such remarks insult children's intelligence. They are more than capable of behaving appropriately in public and at home, although enforcement is required, because they are learning the ways of the world. I saw this at my school, and know of my own knowledge that life can be different.

We have bullies because parents themselves lack self-control, thus modeling the perfect bully. They also allow children to treat others disrespectfully, and it starts very early. By the time teens are harassing gays at school, it's too late, for they already know they can act with impunity.

People will say that I don't understand today's children. But I do, and know that they are the creations of today's parents. Teachers quickly tire of the expectations laid on them by weak parents. Note that many teachers are very young, which means constant recruitment (a huge expense). It also means that our children are, for the most part, being educated by relatively inexperienced staff (a disservice to students). And young teachers lack the benefit of experienced colleagues to mentor them.

In today's schools, much of what I see looks like adults attempting to control chaos. Imagine if teachers were not constantly correcting behavior, or dealing with bedlam in the classroom, or fending off complaints from parents, or being called on the carpet by the principal for upholding standards! They could then be educators, and I might go back to teaching.

About The Author

Mary Jane Wilkie is a music educator and writer. Since 1994, she has taught in private and public schools (California, New York metropolitan area), which experience has brought her in regular contact with the children who are the subject of *Music from the Trenches*. She has taught piano to young children. She has given workshops to classroom teachers who wish to incorporate music into their curriculum, and to music teachers wishing to know about specific music pedagogies.

Ms. Wilkie has been pianist and music director for children's and youth theatre productions, and accompanist at student recitals. As director of Sunday school she has overseen Christmas pageants and other performances by children. She has taught children's theatre to 5- and 6-year olds. She has training in the Kodály and Orff music pedagogies, and holds an M.A. in Musicology from Brooklyn College (City University of New York). She has published articles on music and children.

(E n d n o t e s)

1 Boston Pops Music Director Keith Lockhart, quoted in *Music Educators Journal,* September 1997, vol. 84, no. 2, p. 39.

2 *The Politics,* trans. T.A. Sinclair (Harmondworth: Penguin Classics, revised ed. 1981).

3 Sharon Begley, in "Caveman Crooners May Have Helped Early Humans Survive," *The Wall Street Journal.* 31 March 2006, p. A-11.

4 *The Mozart Effect,* by Don Campbell (Avon, 1997). See especially the portions pertaining to the work of French physician Alfred Tomatis, who has thoroughly explored the hearing phenomenon.

5 For a compilation, see *Spin-Offs: The Extra-Musical Advantages of a Musical Education,* published by United Musical Instruments U.S.A., Inc., 1995.

6 From an address to the National Press Club, as reported in *The Juilliard Journal,* May 1997.

7 Linda Ferreira, quoted in *Choral Journal,* March 1993, vol. 33, no. 8, p. 25.

8 Quoted in *Teaching Music,* February 1997, vol. 4, no. 4, p. 64.

9 *Ibid.,* p. 64.

10 Wilma Machover, in *Sound Choices* (Oxford, 1996), p. 281.

11   Roberta Markel in *Music for Your Child* (Facts on File, 1983), p. 2.

12   Stephen J. Dubner and Steven D. Levitt, "A Star is Made," *The New York Times* 7 May 2006. The authors are quoting the work of Anders Ericsson.

13   *The Singing Neanderthals,* by Stephen Mithen (Harvard University Press, 2006).

14   Quoted in Machover, p. 285.

15   Machover, p. 282.

16   Machover, p. 292.

17   Gary Gelber, in "Psychological Issues Encountered in Gifted Children and Adolescents." *Music and Child Development.* Frank R. Wilson and Franz L. Roehmann, eds., MMB Music, Inc., 1990.

18   Markel, p.69.

19   Elizabeth Jones, "What Children Teach Us About Learning Music," in *Music and Child Development.* MMB Music, Inc. 1990, p. 370.

20   Interviewed in *Teaching Music,* February 1997, vol. 4, No. 4, p. 64.

21   Machover, p. 292.

22   Interviewed in *Teaching Music,* June 1998, vol. 5, No. 6, p. 44.

23   Interviewed in *Teaching Music,* February 1997, vol. 4, No. 4, p. 39.

24   Nelson, Esther L., *Dancing Games for Children of All Ages* (New York, Sterling Publishing Co., Inc., 1973), p. 4.

ENDNOTES

25 Cushman, Kathleen, in "Don't Let the Singing Stop," condensed from *Woman's Day* and printed in *Reader's Digest*, vol. 1422, fall 1993 pp. 167-8.

26 Detailed information about the evolution of instruments can be found in Curt Sachs's *The History of Musical Instruments* (New York, W.W. Norton & Co., Inc., 1940).

27 Mentioned by Donna Brink Fox of the Eastman School of Music, quoted in *CMEA News*, November/December 1997, vol. 51, No. 2, p. 27.

28 Machover, p. 256.

29 One such publication is Larry Fine's *The Piano Book* (Boston, Brookside Press, 1987). See also Chapter 4 in Roberta Markel's book for help in choosing any type of instrument.

30 Markel, p. 98.

31 *Clavier*, vol. 35, No. 6, July/August 1996, p. 18.

32 In *Nurtured by Love*, Sensay Publications, Athens, Ohio, 1983.

33 Gary S. Gelber, "Psychological issues Encountered in Gifted Children and Adolescents," in *Music and Child Development*, p. 272.

34 Markel, p. 26.

35 Brian Rowley, quoted in *Teaching Music*, October 1995, vol. 3, No. 2, p. 44.

36 Chouinard, Yvon. "Patagonia: the Next 100 Years," in *Sacred Trusts*, Michael Katakis, ed. (San Francisco: Mercury House, 1993).

37 Listed in *A Dictionary of Musical Quotations,* compiled by Ian Crofton and Donald Fraser. Schirmer Books, 1985.

38 Randall Dana Ulveland, writing in *Music Educators Journal,* July 1998, vol. 85, no. 1, p. 29.

39 See Patricia Shehan Campbell's book *Music in Childhood* (Schirmer Books, 1995). Ms. Campbell devotes an entire chapter to technology for music instruction.

40 Kenneth H. Phillips, writing in *Teaching Music,* February 1997, vol. 4, no. 4, p. 10.

41 Doreen Rao, writing in *Choral Journal,* March 1989, vol. xxix, no. 8, p. 13.

42 Edwin Gordon in *Learning Sequences in Music* (GIA Publications, 1993), p. 216.

43 Markel, p. 39.

44 Gordon, p. 2. See Oliver Sacks, *Musicophilia,* for cases about persons with unusual processing of music.

45 Campbell, p. 7, citing Howard Gardner.

46 Campbell, p. 7.

47 John A. Sloboda, "Music as a Language," in *Music and Child Development,* p. 29.

48 Healy, Jane M., Ph.D. in *Endangered Minds – why Children Don't Think and What we Can Do about it* (Simon & Schuster, 1990), p. 93.

49 Robert Garfias, "The Processes of Language and Music Acquisition," in *Music and Child Development,* p. 103.

50 Herbert Kupferberg, "The New Sounds of Success in School," *Parade,* 2/28/99, p. 8 [emphasis mine].

ENDNOTES

51   The three mentioned are the most well known methods. Others are Comprehensive Musicianship, the work of Edwin Gordon, the Manhattanville Music Curriculum Project, Music in Education (Yamaha), Education through Music, and the work of Phyllis Weikart. The Suzuki method serves learning in private lessons with a particular instrument.

52   John Feierabend, in *Kódaly Envoy*, Winter 1997, vol. 23, No. 2, p. 8.

53   Linda Swears, in *Teaching the Elementary School Chorus* (Parker Publishing Co., Inc., 1985), p. 161.

54   Grant Newman, in *Teaching Children Music* (Wm. C. Brown, 1979), p. 190.

55   John Feierabend in *Kódaly Envoy*, Winter 1997, vol. 23, No. 2, p. 2.

56   Leslie Guelker-Cone, in *Music Educators Journal*, September 1998, vol. 85, No. 2, p. 17.

57   In *Music Educators Journal*, September 1998, vol. 85, No. 2, p. 6.

58   Described by George DeGraffenreid in *California Music Educators Association News*, November/December 1997, vol. 51, No. 2, p. 32.

59   Doreen Rao, writing in *Choral Journal*, vol. xxix, No. 8, March 1989, p. 13.

60   Kenneth H. Phillips, in *Teaching Music*, February 1997, vol. 4, No. 4, p. 10.

61   For help with this decision, refer to Machover (part Two) and Markel (Chapters 4 and 5).

62   Markel, p. 3.

MUSIC FROM THE TRENCHES

63 Interviewed in *Music Educators Journal,* September 1997, vol. 84, no. 2, p. 39.

64 John M. Feierabend, former President of the Organization of American Kodaly Educators, in *Kodaly Envoy,* Winter 1997, vol. 23, no. 2, p. 7.

65 In *Letters to Malcolm* (Harcourt, Brace & World, Inc., 1963), p. 84.

66 "Religious Music in the Schools," published by the Music Educators National Conference, 1987.

67 *Ibid.,* here quoting Abraham A. Schwadron.

68 *Ibid.*

Made in the USA
Charleston, SC
30 November 2014